SEAMUS HEANEY

Wintering Out

——

ff

faber and faber

First published in 1972
by Faber & Faber Ltd
Bloomsbury House
74–77 Great Russell Street
London WC1B 3DA

Set in Linotype Sabon
Printed and bound in Great Britain by
TJ International Ltd, Padstow, Cornwall

A CIP record for this book
is available from the British Library

ISBN 978–0–571–10158–0

For David Hammond and Michael Longley

This morning from a dewy motorway
I saw the new camp for the internees:
a bomb had left a crater of fresh clay
in the roadside, and over in the trees

machine-gun posts defined a real stockade.
There was that white mist you get on a low ground
and it was déjà-vu, some film made
of Stalag 17, a bad dream with no sound.

Is there a life before death? That's chalked up
on a wall downtown. Competence with pain,
coherent miseries, a bite and sup,
we hug our little destiny again.

Contents

Acknowledgements and Notes

Acknowledgements are due to the editors of the following
magazines where most of these poems appeared, a number of
them in slightly different form:
Aquarius, Atlantis, Criterion (Galway), *The Critical
Quarterly, Gown, The Guardian, Hibernia, Honest
Ulsterman, Irish Press, Irish Times, Listener, The Malahat
Review, Michigan Quarterly Review, New Statesman,
Occident, Phoenix, Poetry* (Chicago), *Poetry Book Society
Supplement, Stand, Threshold*;
and to the editor of *Modern Poets in Focus 2* (Corgi) and *The
Young British Poets* (Chatto).
'Fireside' and Sections II and V of 'Summer Home' (originally
entitled 'Home' and 'Aubade') © *The New Yorker*, 1971.
'Land', 'Servant Boy' and Sections III and IV of 'Summer
Home' appeared as broadsheets from Poem of the Month, The
Red Hanrahan Press and Tara Telephone respectively.
'Bye-Child' appeared in *Twelve to Twelve* (Camden Festival,
1970); 'Servant Boy' appeared in *Responses* (National Book
League and Poetry Society, 1971).
'The Tollund Man' and 'Nerthus' originated from a reading of
P. V. Glob's *The Bog People* (Faber).
'Maighdean Mara' is the Irish for 'mermaid'.

PART ONE

Fodder

Or, as we said,
fother, I open
my arms for it
again. But first

to draw from the tight
vise of a stack
the weathered eaves
of the stack itself

falling at your feet,
last summer's tumbled
swathes of grass
and meadowsweet

multiple as loaves
and fishes, a bundle
tossed over half-doors
or into mucky gaps.

These long nights
I would pull hay
for comfort, anything
to bed the stall.

Bog Oak

A carter's trophy
Split for rafters,
a cobwebbed, black,
long-seasoned rib

under the first thatch.
I might tarry
with the moustached
dead, the creel-fillers,

or eavesdrop on
their hopeless wisdom
as a blow-down of smoke
struggles over the half-door

and mizzling rain
blurs the far end
of the cart track.
The softening ruts

lead back to no
'oak groves', no
cutters of mistletoe
in the green clearings.

Perhaps I just make out
Edmund Spenser,
dreaming sunlight,
encroached upon by

geniuses who creep
'out of every corner
of the woodes and glennes'
towards watercress and carrion.

Anahorish

My 'place of clear water',
the first hill in the world
where springs washed into
the shiny grass

and darkened cobbles
in the bed of the lane.
Anahorish, soft gradient
of consonant, vowel-meadow,

after-image of lamps
swung through the yards
on winter evenings.
With pails and barrows

those mound-dwellers
go waist-deep in mist
to break the light ice
at wells and dunghills.

Servant Boy

He is wintering out
the back-end of a bad year,
swinging a hurricane-lamp
through some outhouse;

a jobber among shadows.
Old work-whore, slave-
blood, who stepped fair-hills
under each bidder's eye

and kept your patience
and your counsel, how
you draw me into
your trail. Your trail

broken from haggard to stable,
a straggle of fodder
stiffened on snow,
comes first-footing

the back doors of the little
barons: resentful
and impenitent,
carrying the warm eggs.

The Last Mummer

I

Carries a stone in his pocket,
an ash-plant under his arm.

Moves out of the fog
on the lawn, pads up the terrace.

The luminous screen in the corner
has them charmed in a ring

so he stands a long time behind them.
St. George, Beelzebub and Jack Straw

can't be conjured from mist.
He catches the stick in his fist

and, shrouded, starts beating
the bars of the gate.

His boots crack the road. The stone
clatters down off the slates.

II

He came trammelled
in the taboos of the country

picking a nice way through
the long toils of blood

[8]

and feuding.
His tongue went whoring

among the civil tongues,
he had an eye for weather-eyes

at cross-roads and lane-ends
and could don manners

at a flutter of curtains.
His straw mask and hunch were fabulous

disappearing beyond the lamplit
slabs of a yard.

III

You dream a cricket in the hearth
and cockroach on the floor,

a line of mummers
marching out the door

as the lamp flares in the draught.
Melted snow off their feet

leaves you in peace.
Again an old year dies

on your hearthstone, for good luck.
The moon's host elevated

in a monstrance of holly trees,
he makes dark tracks, who had

untousled a first dewy path
into the summer grazing.

Land

I stepped it, perch by perch.
Unbraiding rushes and grass
I opened my right-of-way
through old bottoms and sowed-out ground
and gathered stones off the ploughing
to raise a small cairn.
Cleaned out the drains, faced the hedges
often got up at dawn
to walk the outlying fields.

I composed habits for those acres
so that my last look would be
neither gluttonous nor starved.
I was ready to go anywhere.

II

This is in place of what I would leave
plaited and branchy
on a long slope of stubble:

a woman of old wet leaves,
rush-bands and thatcher's scollops,
stooked loosely, her breasts an open-work

of new straw and harvest bows.
Gazing out past
the shifting hares.

I sense the pads
unfurling under grass and clover:

if I lie with my ear
in this loop of silence

long enough, thigh-bone
and shoulder against the phantom ground,

I expect to pick up
a small drumming

and must not be surprised
in bursting air

to find myself snared, swinging
an ear-ring of sharp wire.

Gifts of Rain

Cloudburst and steady downpour now
for days.
             Still mammal,
straw-footed on the mud,
he begins to sense weather
by his skin.

A nimble snout of flood
licks over stepping stones
and goes uprooting.
                    He fords
his life by sounding.
                    Soundings.

A man wading lost fields
breaks the pane of flood:

a flower of mud-
water blooms up to his reflection

like a cut swaying
its red spoors through a basin.

His hands grub
where the spade has uncastled

sunken drills, an atlantis
he depends on. So

he is hooped to where he planted
and sky and ground

are running naturally among his arms
that grope the cropping land.

III

When rains were gathering
there would be an all-night
roaring off the ford.
Their world-schooled ear

could monitor the usual
confabulations, the race
slabbering past the gable,
the Moyola harping on

its gravel beds:
all spouts by daylight
brimmed with their own airs
and overflowed each barrel

in long tresses.
I cock my ear
at an absence –
in the shared calling of blood

arrives my need
for antediluvian lore.
Soft voices of the dead
are whispering by the shore

that I would question
(and for my children's sake)
about crops rotted, river mud
glazing the baked clay floor.

IV

The tawny guttural water
spells itself: Moyola
is its own score and consort,

bedding the locale
in the utterance,
reed music, an old chanter

breathing its mists
through vowels and history.
A swollen river,

a mating call of sound
rises to pleasure me, Dives,
hoarder of common ground.

[15]

Toome

My mouth holds round
the soft blastings,
Toome, Toome,
as under the dislodged

slab of the tongue
I push into a souterrain
prospecting what new
in a hundred centuries'

loam, flints, musket-balls,
fragmented ware,
torcs and fish-bones
till I am sleeved in

alluvial mud that shelves
suddenly under
bogwater and tributaries,
and elvers tail my hair.

Broagh

Riverback, the long rigs
ending in broad docken
and a canopied pad
down to the ford.

The garden mould
bruised easily, the shower
gathering in your heelmark
was the black O

in *Broagh*,
its low tattoo
among the windy boortrees
and rhubarb-blades

ended almost
suddenly, like that last
gh the strangers found
difficult to manage.

Oracle

Hide in the hollow trunk
of the willow tree,
its listening familiar,
until, as usual, they
cuckoo your name
across the fields.
You can hear them
draw the poles of stiles
as they approach
calling you out:
small mouth and ear
in a woody cleft,
lobe and larynx
of the mossy places.

The Backward Look

A stagger in air
as if a language
failed, a sleight
of wing.

A snipe's bleat is fleeing
its nesting ground
into dialect,
into variants,

transliterations whirr
on the nature reserves —
little goat of the air,
of the evening,

little goat of the frost.
It is his tail-feathers
drumming elegies
in the slipstream

of wild goose
and yellow bittern
as he corkscrews away
into the vaults

that we live off, his flight
through the sniper's eyrie,
over twilit earthworks
and wall-steads,

disappearing among
gleanings and leavings
in the combs
of a fieldworker's archive.

Traditions

For Tom Flanagan

I

Our guttural muse
was bulled long ago
by the alliterative tradition,
her uvula grows

vestigial, forgotten
like the coccyx
or a Brigid's Cross
yellowing in some outhouse

while custom, that 'most
sovereign mistress',
beds us down into
the British isles.

II

We are to be proud
of our Elizabethan English:
'varsity', for example,
is grass-roots stuff with us;

we 'deem' or we 'allow'
when we suppose
and some cherished archaisms
are correct Shakespearean.

Not to speak of the furled
consonants of lowlanders
shuttling obstinately
between bawn and mossland.

III

MacMorris, gallivanting
round the Globe, whinged
to courtier and groundling
who had heard tell of us

as going very bare
of learning, as wild hares,
as anatomies of death:
'What ish my nation?'

And sensibly, though so much
later, the wandering Bloom
replied, 'Ireland,' said Bloom,
'I was born here. Ireland.'

A New Song

I met a girl from Derrygarve
And the name, a lost potent musk,
Recalled the river's long swerve,
A kingfisher's blue bolt at dusk

And stepping stones like black molars
Sunk in the ford, the shifty glaze
Of the whirlpool, the Moyola
Pleasuring beneath alder trees.

And Derrygarve, I thought, was just,
Vanished music, twilit water,
A smooth libation of the past
Poured by this chance vestal daughter.

But now our river tongues must rise
From licking deep in native haunts
To flood, with vowelling embrace,
Demesnes staked out in consonants.

And Castledawson we'll enlist
And Upperlands, each planted bawn –
Like bleaching-greens resumed by grass –
A vocable, as rath and bullaun.

The Other Side

Thigh-deep in sedge and marigolds
a neighbour laid his shadow
on the stream, vouching

'It's poor as Lazarus, that ground,'
and brushed away
among the shaken leafage:

I lay where his lea sloped
to meet our fallow,
nested on moss and rushes,

my ear swallowing
his fabulous, biblical dismissal,
that tongue of chosen people.

When he would stand like that
on the other side, white-haired,
swinging his blackthorn

at the marsh weeds,
he prophesied above our scraggy acres,
then turned away

towards his promised furrows
on the hill, a wake of pollen
drifting to our bank, next season's tares.

II

For days we would rehearse
each patriarchal dictum:
Lazarus, the Pharaoh, Solomon

and David and Goliath rolled
magnificently, like loads of hay
too big for our small lanes,

or faltered on a rut —
'Your side of the house, I believe,
hardly rule by the book at all.'

His brain was a whitewashed kitchen
hung with texts, swept tidy
as the body o' the kirk.

III

Then sometimes when the rosary was dragging
mournfully on in the kitchen
we would hear his step round the gable

though not until after the litany
would the knock come to the door
and the casual whistle strike up

on the doorstep. 'A right-looking night,'
he might say, 'I was dandering by
and says I, I might as well call.'

But now I stand behind him
in the dark yard, in the moan of prayers.
He puts a hand in a pocket

or taps a little tune with the blackthorn
shyly, as if he were party to
lovemaking or a stranger's weeping.

Should I slip away, I wonder,
or go up and touch his shoulder
and talk about the weather

or the price of grass-seed?

The Wool Trade

'How different are the words "home",
"Christ", "ale", "master", on his
lips and on mine.' STEPHEN DEDALUS

'The wool trade' — the phrase
Rambled warm as a fleece

Out of his hoard.
To shear, to bale and bleach and card

Unwound from the spools
Of his vowels

And square-set men in tunics
Who plied soft names like Bruges

In their talk, merchants
Back from the Netherlands:

O all the hamlets where
Hills and flocks and streams conspired

To a language of waterwheels,
A lost syntax of looms and spindles,

How they hang
Fading, in the gallery of the tongue!

And I must talk of tweed,
A stiff cloth with flecks like blood.

[27]

Linen Town
High Street, Belfast, 1786

It's twenty to four
By the public clock. A cloaked rider
Clops off into an entry

Coming perhaps from the Linen Hall
Or Cornmarket
Where, the civic print unfrozen,

In twelve years' time
They hanged young McCracken –
This lownecked belle and tricorned fop's

Still flourish undisturbed
By the swinging tongue of his body.
Pen and ink, water tint

Fence and fetch us in
Under bracketed tavern signs,
The edged gloom of arcades.

It's twenty to four
On one of the last afternoons
Of reasonable light.

Smell the tidal Lagan:
Take a last turn
In the tang of possibility.

A Northern Hoard

And some in dreams assured were
Of the Spirit that plagued us so

I. ROOTS

Leaf membranes lid the window.
In the streetlamp's glow
Your body's moonstruck
To drifted barrow, sunk glacial rock.

And all shifts dreamily as you keen
Far off, turning from the din
Of gunshot, siren and clucking gas
Out there beyond each curtained terrace

Where the fault is opening. The touch of love,
Your warmth heaving to the first move,
Grows helpless in our old Gomorrah.
We petrify or uproot now.

I'll dream it for us before dawn
When the pale sniper steps down
And I approach the shrub.
I've soaked by moonlight in tidal blood

A mandrake, lodged human fork,
Earth sac, limb of the dark;
And I wound its damp smelly loam
And stop my ears against the scream.

[29]

2. NO MAN'S LAND

I deserted, shut out
their wounds' fierce awning,
those palms like streaming webs.

Must I crawl back now,
spirochete, abroad between
shred-hung wire and thorn,
to confront my smeared doorstep
and what lumpy dead?
Why do I unceasingly
arrive late to condone
infected sutures
and ill-knit bone?

3. STUMP

I am riding to plague again.
Sometimes under a sooty wash
From the grate in the burnt-out gable
I see the needy in a small pow-wow.
What do I say if they wheel out their dead?
I'm cauterized, a black stump of home.

4. NO SANCTUARY

It's Hallowe'en. The turnip-man's lopped head
Blazes at us through split bottle glass
And fumes and swims up like a wrecker's lantern.

Death mask of harvest, mocker at All Souls
With scorching smells, red dog's eyes in the night –
We ring and stare into unhallowed light.

5. TINDER

We picked flints,
Pale and dirt-veined,

So small finger and thumb
Ached around them;

Cold beads of history and home
We fingered, a cave-mouth flame

Of leaf and stick
Trembling at the mind's wick.

We clicked stone on stone
That sparked a weak flame-pollen

And failed, our knuckle joints
Striking as often as the flints.

What did we know then
Of tinder, charred linen and iron,

Huddled at dusk in a ring,
Our fists shut, our hope shrunken?

What could strike a blaze
From our dead igneous days?

Now we squat on cold cinder,
Red-eyed, after the flames' soft thunder

And our thoughts settle like ash.
We face the tundra's whistling brush

With new history, flint and iron,
Cast-offs, scraps, nail, canine.

Midnight

Since the professional wars —
Corpse and carrion
Paling in rain —
The wolf has died out

In Ireland. The packs
Scoured parkland and moor
Till a Quaker buck and his dogs
Killed the last one

In some scraggy waste of Kildare.
The wolfhound was crossed
With inferior strains,
Forests coopered to wine casks.

Rain on the roof to-night
Sogs turf-banks and heather,
Sets glinting outcrops
Of basalt and granite,

Drips to the moss of bare boughs.
The old dens are soaking.
The pads are lost or
Retrieved by small vermin

That glisten and scut.
Nothing is panting, lolling,
Vapouring. The tongue's
Leashed in my throat.

The Tollund Man

I

Some day I will go to Aarhus
To see his peat-brown head,
The mild pods of his eye-lids,
His pointed skin cap.

In the flat country nearby
Where they dug him out,
His last gruel of winter seeds
Caked in his stomach,

Naked except for
The cap, noose and girdle,
I will stand a long time.
Bridegroom to the goddess,

She tightened her torc on him
And opened her fen,
Those dark juices working
Him to a saint's kept body,

Trove of the turfcutters'
Honeycombed workings.
Now his stained face
Reposes at Aarhus.

I could risk blasphemy,
Consecrate the cauldron bog
Our holy ground and pray
Him to make germinate

The scattered, ambushed
Flesh of labourers,
Stockinged corpses
Laid out in the farmyards,

Tell-tale skin and teeth
Flecking the sleepers
Of four young brothers, trailed
For miles along the lines.

III

Something of his sad freedom
As he rode the tumbril
Should come to me, driving,
Saying the names

Tollund, Grabaulle, Nebelgard,
Watching the pointing hands
Of country people,
Not knowing their tongue.

Out there in Jutland
In the old man-killing parishes
I will feel lost,
Unhappy and at home.

Nerthus

For beauty, say an ash-fork staked in peat,
Its long grains gathering to the gouged split;

A seasoned, unsleeved taker of the weather,
Where kesh and loaning finger out to heather.

Cairn-maker

For Barrie Cooke

He robbed the stones' nests, uncradled
As he orphaned and betrothed rock
To rock: his unaccustomed hand
Went chambering upon hillock

And bogland. Clamping, balancing,
That whole day spent in the Burren,
He did not find and add to them
But piled up small cairn after cairn

And dressed some stones with his own mark.
Which he tells of with almost fear;
And of strange affiliation
To what was touched and handled there,

Unexpected hives and castlings
Pennanted now, claimed by no hand:
Rush and ladysmock, heather-bells
Blowing in each aftermath of wind.

Navvy

The moleskins stiff as bark,
the drill grafting his wrists
to the shale:
where the surface is weavy

and the camber tilts
in the slow lane, he stands
waving you down. The morass
the macadam snakes over

swallowed his yellow bulldozer
four years ago, laying it down
with lake-dwellings and dug-outs,
pike-shafts, axe-heads, bone pins,

all he is indifferent to.
He has not relented
under weather or insults,
my brother and keeper

plugged to the hard-core,
picking along
the welted, stretchmarked
curve of the world.

Veteran's Dream

Mr Dickson, my neighbour,
Who saw the last cavalry charge
Of the war and got the first gas
Walks with a limp

Into his helmet and khaki.
He notices indifferently
The gas has yellowed his buttons
And near his head

Horses plant their shods.
His real fear is gangrene.
He wakes with his hand to the scar
And they do their white magic

Where he lies
On cankered ground,
A scatter of maggots, busy
In the trench of his wound.

Augury

The fish faced into the current,
Its mouth agape,
Its whole head opened like a valve.
You said 'It's diseased.'

A pale crusted sore
Turned like a coin
And wound to the bottom,
Unsettling silt off a weed.

We hang charmed
On the trembling catwalk:
What can fend us now
Can soothe the hurt eye

Of the sun,
Unpoison great lakes,
Turn back
The rat on the road.

PART TWO

Wedding Day

I am afraid.
Sound has stopped in the day
And the images reel over
And over. Why all those tears,

The wild grief on his face
Outside the taxi? The sap
Of mourning rises
In our waving guests.

You sing behind the tall cake
Like a deserted bride
Who persists, demented,
And goes through the ritual.

When I went to the gents
There was a skewered heart
And a legend of love. Let me
sleep on your breast to the airport.

Mother of the Groom

What she remembers
Is his glistening back
In the bath, his small boots
In the ring of boots at her feet.

Hands in her voided lap,
She hears a daughter welcomed.
It's as if he kicked when lifted
And slipped her soapy hold.

Once soap would ease off
The wedding ring
That's bedded forever now
In her clapping hand.

Summer Home

I

Was it wind off the dumps
or something in heat

dogging us, the summer gone sour,
a fouled nest incubating somewhere?

Whose fault, I wondered, inquisitor
of the possessed air.

To realize suddenly,
whip off the mat

that was larval, moving —
and scald, scald, scald.

II

Bushing the door, my arms full
of wild cherry and rhododendron,
I hear her small lost weeping
through the hall, that bells and hoarsens
on my name, my name.

O love, here is the blame.

The loosened flowers between us
gather in, compose
for a May altar of sorts.
These frank and falling blooms
soon taint to a sweet chrism.

Attend. Anoint the wound.

III

O we tented our wound all right
under the homely sheet

and lay as if the cold flat of a blade
had winded us.

More and more I postulate
thick healings, like now

as you bend in the shower
water lives down the tilting stoups of your breasts.

IV

With a final
unmusical drive
long grains begin
to open and split

ahead and once more
we sap
the white, trodden
path to the heart.

V

My children weep out the hot foreign night.
We walk the floor, my foul mouth takes it out
On you and we lie stiff till dawn
Attends the pillow, and the maize, and vine

That holds its filling burden to the light.
Yesterday rocks sang when we tapped
Stalactites in the cave's old, dripping dark —
Our love calls tiny as a tuning fork.

Serenades

The Irish nightingale
Is a sedge-warbler,
A little bird with a big voice
Kicking up a racket all night.

Not what you'd expect
From the musical nation.
I haven't even heard one —
Nor an owl, for that matter.

My serenades have been
The broken voice of a crow
In a draught or a dream,
The wheeze of bats

Or the ack-ack
Of the tramp corncrake
Lost in a no man's land
Between combines and chemicals.

So fill the bottles, love,
Leave them inside their cots.
And if they do wake us, well,
So would the sedge-warbler.

Somnambulist

Nestrobber's hands
and a face in its net of gossamer;

he came back weeping
to unstarch the pillow

and freckle her sheets
with tiny yolk.

A Winter's Tale

A pallor in the headlights'
Range wavered and disappeared.
Weeping, blood bright from her cuts
Where she'd fled the hedged and wired
Road, they eyed her nakedness
Astray among the cattle
At first light. Lanterns, torches
And the searchers' gay babble
She eluded earlier:
Now her own people only
Closed around her dazed whimper
With rugs, dressings and brandy –
Conveying maiden daughter
Back to family hearth and floor.
Why run, our lovely daughter,
Bare-breasted from our door?

Still, like good luck, she returned.
Some nights, crossing the thresholds
Of empty homes, she warmed
Her dewy roundings and folds
To sleep in the chimney nook.
After all, they were neighbours.
As neighbours, when they came back
Surprised but unmalicious
Greetings passed
Between them. She was there first
And so appeared no haunter

But, making all comers guests,
She stirred as from a winter
Sleep. Smiled. Uncradled her breasts.

Shore Woman

Man to the hills, woman to the shore.

Gaelic proverb

I have crossed the dunes with their whistling bent
Where dry loose sand was riddling round the air
And I'm walking the firm margin. White pocks
Of cockle, blanched roofs of clam and oyster
Hoard the moonlight, woven and unwoven
Off the bay. At the far rocks
A pale sud comes and goes.

Under boards the mackerel slapped to death
Yet still we took them in at every cast,
Stiff flails of cold convulsed with their first breath.
My line plumbed certainly the undertow,
Loaded against me once I went to draw
And flashed and fattened up towards the light.
He was all business in the stern. I called
'This is so easy that it's hardly right,'
But he unhooked and coped with frantic fish
Without speaking. Then suddenly it lulled,
We'd crossed where they were running, the line rose
Like a let-down and I was conscious
How far we'd drifted out beyond the head.
'Count them up at your end,' was all he said
Before I saw the porpoises' thick backs
Cartwheeling like the flywheels of the tide,
Soapy and shining. To have seen a hill
Splitting the water could not have numbed me more
Than the close irruption of that school,
Tight viscous muscle, hooped from tail to snout,

[54]

Each one revealed complete as it bowled out
And under.
                    They will attack a boat.
I knew it and I asked him to put in
But he would not, declared it was a yarn
My people had been fooled by far too long
And he would prove it now and settle it.
Maybe he shrank when those sloped oily backs
Propelled towards us: I lay and screamed
Under splashed brine in an open rocking boat
Feeling each dunt and slither through the timber,
Sick at their huge pleasures in the water.

I sometimes walk this strand for thanksgiving
Or maybe it's to get away from him
Skittering his spit across the stove. Here
Is the taste of safety, the shelving sand
Harbours no worse than razor-shell or crab –
Though my father recalls carcasses of whales
Collapsed and gasping, right up to the dunes.
But to-night such moving sinewed dreams lie out
In darker fathoms, far beyond the head.
Astray upon a debris of scrubbed shells
Between parched dunes and salivating wave,
I have rights on this fallow avenue,
A membrane between moonlight and my shadow.

Maighdean Mara

For Seán Oh-Eocha

I

She sleeps now, her cold breasts
Dandled by undertow,
Her hair lifted and laid.
Undulant slow seawracks
Cast about shin and thigh,
Bangles of wort, drifting
Liens catch, dislodge gently.

This is the great first sleep
Of homecoming, eight
Land years between hearth and
Bed steeped and dishevelled.
Her magic garment al-
most ocean-tinctured still.

II

He stole her garments as
She combed her hair: follow
Was all that she could do.
He hid it in the eaves
And charmed her there, four walls,
Warm floor, man-love nightly
In earshot of the waves.

She suffered milk and birth –
She had no choice – conjured
Patterns of home and drained

The tidesong from her voice.
Then the thatcher came and stuck
Her garment in a stack.
Children carried tales back.

III

In night air, entering
Foam, she wrapped herself
With smoke-reeks from his thatch,
Straw-musts and films of mildew.
She dipped his secret there
Forever and uncharmed

Accents of fisher wives,
The dead hold of bedrooms,
Dread of the night and morrow,
Her children's brush and combs.
She sleeps now, her cold breasts
Dandled by undertow.

Limbo

Fishermen at Ballyshannon
Netted an infant last night
Along with the salmon.
An illegitimate spawning,

A small one thrown back
To the waters. But I'm sure
As she stood in the shallows
Ducking him tenderly

Till the frozen knobs of her wrists
Were dead as the gravel,
He was a minnow with hooks
Tearing her open.

She waded in under
The sign of her cross.
He was hauled in with the fish.
Now limbo will be

A cold glitter of souls
Through some far briny zone.
Even Christ's palms, unhealed,
Smart and cannot fish there.

Bye-Child

He was discovered in the henhouse
where she had confined him. He was
incapable of saying anything.

When the lamp glowed,
A yolk of light
In their back window,
The child in the outhouse
Put his eye to a chink —

Little henhouse boy,
Sharp-faced as new moons
Remembered, your photo still
Glimpsed like a rodent
On the floor of my mind,

Little moon man,
Kennelled and faithful
At the foot of the yard,
Your frail shape, luminous,
Weightless, is stirring the dust,

The cobwebs, old droppings
Under the roosts
And dry smells from scraps
She put through your trapdoor
Morning and evening.

After those footsteps, silence;
Vigils, solitudes, fasts,

Unchristened tears,
A puzzled love of the light.
But now you speak at last

With a remote mime
Of something beyond patience,
Your gaping wordless proof
Of lunar distances
Travelled beyond love.

Good-night

A latch lifting, an edged den of light
Opens across the yard. Out of the low door
They stoop into the honeyed corridor,
Then walk straight through the wall of the dark.

A puddle, cobble-stones, jambs and doorstep
Are set steady in a block of brightness.
Till she strides in again beyond her shadows
And cancels everything behind her.

First Calf

It's a long time since I saw
The afterbirth strung on the hedge
As if the wind smarted
And streamed bloodshot tears.

Somewhere about the cow stands
With her head almost outweighing
Her tense sloped neck,
The calf hard at her udder.

The shallow bowls of her eyes
Tilt membrane and fluid.
The warm plaque of her snout gathers
A growth round moist nostrils.

Her hide stays warm in the wind.
Her wide eyes read nothing.
The semaphores of hurt
Swaddle and flap on a bush.

May

When I looked down from the bridge
Trout were flipping the sky
Into smithereens, the stones
Of the wall warmed me.

Wading green stems, lugs of leaf
That untangle and bruise
(Their tiny gushers of juice)
My toecaps sparkle now

Over the soft fontanel
Of Ireland. I should wear
Hide shoes, the hair next my skin,
For walking this ground:

Wasn't there a spa-well,
Its coping grassy, pendent?
And then the spring issuing
Right across the tarmac.

I'm out to find that village,
Its low sills fragrant
With ladysmock and celandine,
Marshlights in the summer dark.

Fireside

Always there would be stories of lights
hovering among bushes or at the foot
of a meadow; maybe a goat with cold horns
pluming into the moon; a tingle of chains

on the midnight road. And then maybe
word would come round of that watery
art, the lamping of fishes, and I'd be
mooning my flashlamp on the licked black pelt

of the stream, my left arm splayed to take
a heavy pour and run of the current
occluding the net. Was that the beam
buckling over an eddy or a gleam

of the fabulous? Steady the light
and come to your senses, they're saying good-night.

Dawn

Somebody lets up a blind.
The shrub at the window
Glitters, a mint of green leaves
Pitched and tossed.

When we stopped for lights
In the centre, pigeons were down
On the street, a scatter
Of cobbles, clucking and settling.

We went at five miles an hour.
A tut-tutting colloquy
Was in session, scholars
Arguing through until morning

In a Pompeian silence.
The dummies watched from the window
Displays as we slipped to the sea.
I got away out by myself

On a scurf of winkles and cockles
And found myself suddenly
Unable to move without crunching
Acres of their crisp delicate turrets.

Travel

Oxen supporting their heads
into the afternoon sun,
melons studding the hill like brass:

who reads into distances reads
beyond us, our sleeping children
and the dust settling in scorched grass.

Westering

In California

I sit under Rand McNally's
'Official Map of the Moon' —
The colour of frogskin,
Its enlarged pores held

Open and one called
'Pitiscus' at eye level —
Recalling the last night
In Donegal, my shadow

Neat upon the whitewash
From her bony shine,
The cobbles of the yard
Lit pale as eggs.

Summer had been a free fall
Ending there,
The empty amphitheatre
Of the west. Good Friday

We had started out
Past shopblinds drawn on the afternoon.
Cars stilled outside still churches,
Bikes tilting to a wall;

We drove by,
A dwindling interruption
As clappers smacked
On a bare altar

And congregations bent
To the studded crucifix.
What nails dropped out that hour?
Roads unreeled, unreeled

Falling light as casts
Laid down
On shining waters.
Under the moon's stigmata

Six thousand miles away,
I imagine untroubled dust,
A loosening gravity,
Christ weighing by his hands.